Grisly Gooey Grimy Jokes Facts and Rhymes for Kids

Single Drop Publishing

October 22, 2022

Copyright Bonnie Ferrante

ISBN 978-1-928064-64-0

"Stop talking," said my mother.
"You have a potty mouth."
"Be quiet," said my father.
"You have a naughty mouth."
"Whisper," said my sister.
"Tell me a tongue twister."
"One that's muddy," said my buddy.
"Don't be a fuddy-duddy."
So I looked in this book
and we laughed until we shook.
There were dirty, silly jokes,
facts, and riddles that I spoke.
Pretty soon my stuffy folks
changed and started to coax
for more,
yes more.
Now I'll never be a bore
with my naughty,
potty mouth.

Why did the frustrated skunk lift his tail?

He wanted to raise a stink.

What happened to the germs when the sanitizer told a joke?

They died laughing.

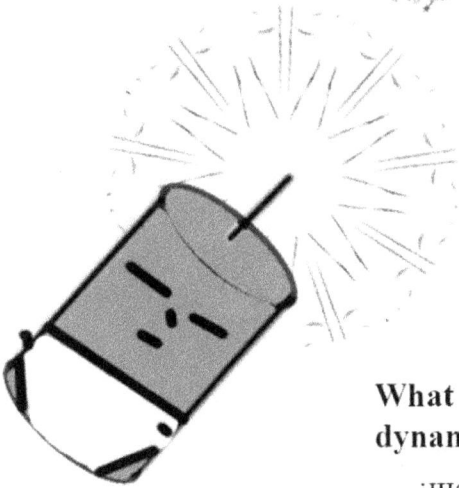

What do you play with dynamite in a diaper?

Pee-ka-boom!

NASTY FACTS

A Toilet Timeline

In 315 AD Romans had public toilets. They wiped themselves with a sponge stuck to the end of a stick. They shared this sponge! Yuck!

In Medieval England people emptied their potties out the window. Walkers ahd to jump out of the way. "Look out below!"

Castles had a room that stuck out over the moat. There was a hole in the floor to use as a toilet. No wonder no one swam in the moat.

In 1592, Sir John Harrington invented the first flush toilet with the water stored in a tank above. Even though it worked well, it didn't become popular.

In 1861, Thomas Crapper built several lavatories in British castles. (That was his real name.)

In 1865 Britain made sewers to keep drinking water clean and free of disease.

In the 1900s, flush toilets and toilet paper were invented. Hurrah!

Take Me Out to the City Dump
(to the tune of Ballgame)

Take me out to the city dump,
Then we can watch the bear.
Eating old peanuts and cracker
jack,
Chewing on everything there.
He will dig, dig, dig, for the best
trash
Until we catch his eye.
Then it's quick get into the car,
Or today's the day we die.

Breakfast with My Baby Brother (to the tune of "I Saw Three Ships Come Sailing In")

I watched my brother eat his food,
at breakfast time, at breakfast time.
It completely changed my mood,
on Saturday in the morning.
He poured his juice onto his bread,
at breakfast time, at breakfast time.
He rubbed grape jelly on his head,
on Saturday in the morning.
The food dripped down on to his clothes,
at breakfast time, at breakfast time,
'til he was covered head to toes,
on Saturday in the morning.
He threw his plate upon the floor,
at breakfast time, at breakfast time,
then shouted out, "More, more, more",
on Saturday in the morning.
He was such a grotesque sight,
at breakfast time, at breakfast time,
I totally lost my appetite,
on Saturday in the morning.

NASTY FACT

Whose food is better after he poops it out than when he first eats it?

An **earthworm** eats 5 tons of soil in a year and makes it better in the process.

My poop is better than your poop.

How did the chihuahua express his excitement?

Yip. Pee. Yip. Pee.

No Apples for the Teacher

There's a grocer on our street.
He's a very strange ghoul.
He sells gross things to eat
That I like to take to school.
I give them to my teacher,
Lleave them on his desk.
But he only takes a tiny bite
And tucks away the rest.
He tells me,
"Thank you for the beetle pie
But I'm full up from brunch.
I'll pack away the snake gut soup.
I'm saving it for lunch.
Grease jam with black fish eyes,
I'll give that to my wife.
Spider chips and goat snot spread,
I'll need to have a knife.
But thank so much for all these things.
I loved the mandrake root,
But maybe some time you could bring
A simple cheese and fruit."

Why doesn't Q like its place in the alphabet?

Because it follows Pee.

Why did the banker sit on his money?

to protect his bottom dollar.

Why did the pig cover himself with mud?

He didn't want to be bacon in the sun.

Better than sunscreen.

The Little Skunk's Hole
(traditional)

I stuck my head
In the little skunk's hole
And the little skunk said,
"Well, bless my soul!
Take it out! Take it out!
Take it out! Remove it!"

I didn't take it out
And the little skunk said,
"If you don't take it out,
You'll wish you had,
Take it out! Take it out!"
Phew! I removed it!

NASTY FACT

What long-eared furry
pet needs to eat its
own poop?

Rabbit's food is not
processed well the
first time through
its body. It needs
to eat the poop in
order to get all the
nutrients.

Mmm.
Tastes
like
carrots.

Why did the billiard player scrub his cue?

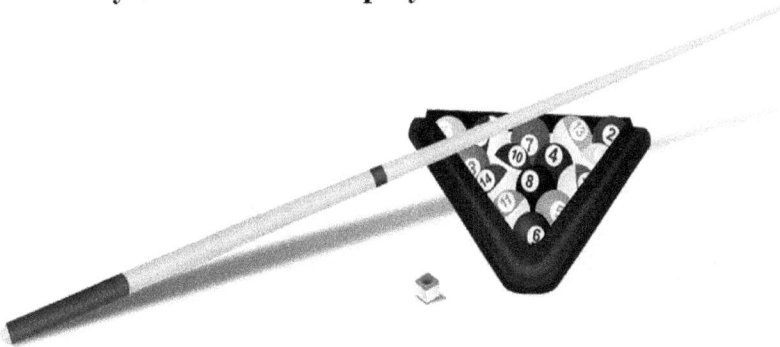

He didn't want to play dirty pool.

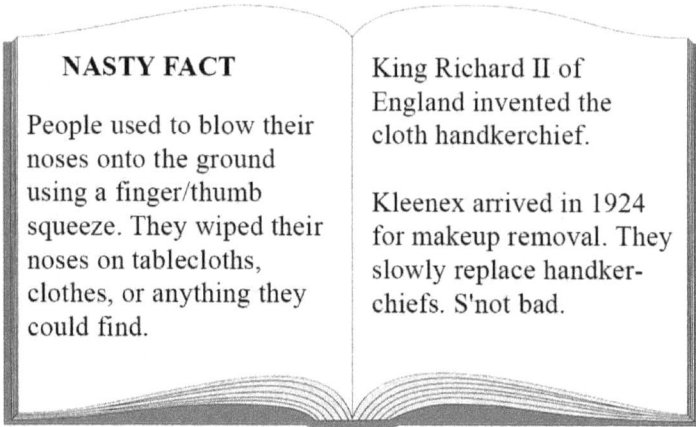

NASTY FACT

People used to blow their noses onto the ground using a finger/thumb squeeze. They wiped their noses on tablecloths, clothes, or anything they could find.

King Richard II of England invented the cloth handkerchief.

Kleenex arrived in 1924 for makeup removal. They slowly replace handkerchiefs. S'not bad.

Why wouldn't the sick athlete throw the javelin?

He didn't want to hurl.

Why did the rock star's fans have wet pants?

Because they were group-pees.

Solomon Grundy

Solomon Grundy, born on Monday,
Christened on Tuesday, Married on
Wednesday,
Took ill on Thursday, Worse on Friday,
Died on Saturday, Buried on Sunday,
This is the end of Solomon Grundy.

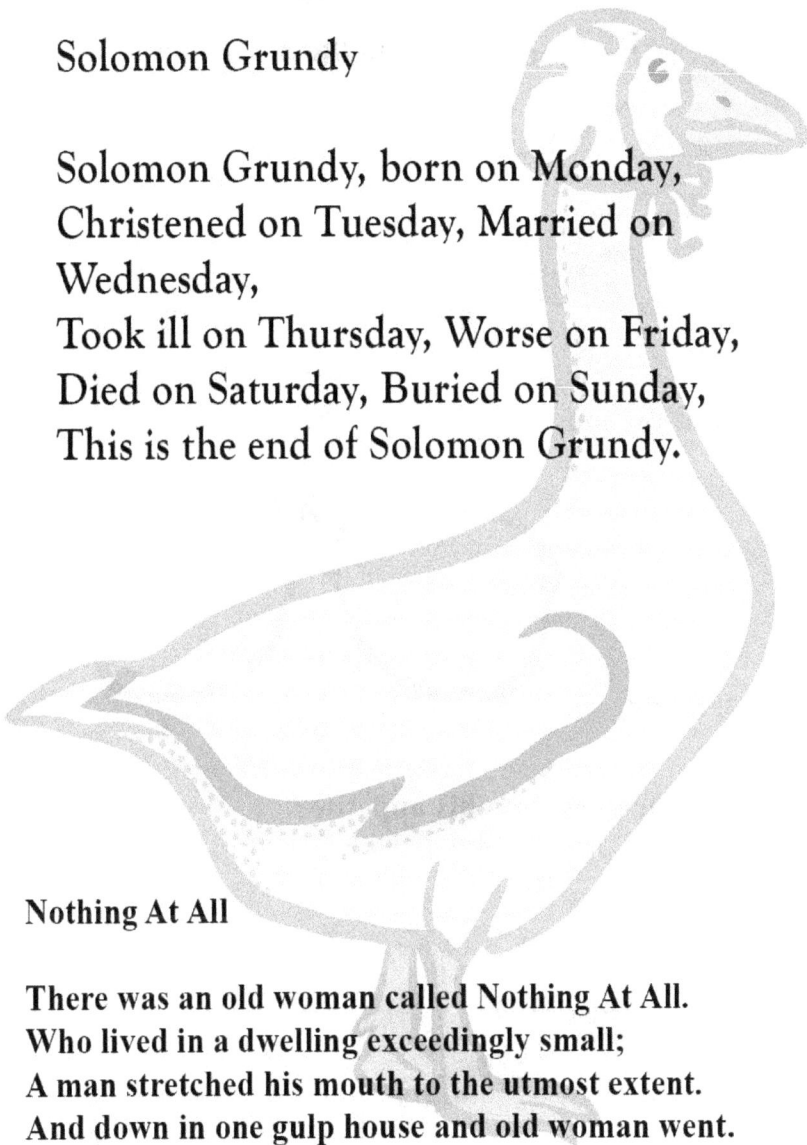

Nothing At All

There was an old woman called Nothing At All.
Who lived in a dwelling exceedingly small;
A man stretched his mouth to the utmost extent.
And down in one gulp house and old woman went.

Mother Goose

Why did the grocer refuse to lift the steak?

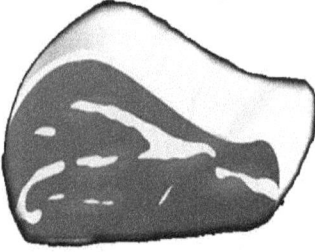

He didn't want to up chuck.

What did the mud wrestler give the optometrist?

A dirty look.

Why did the guest lose his appetite?

Because the host cut the cheese.

Boom! Boom! (traditional)

Refrain
Boom, boom, ain't it great to be crazy!
Boom, boom, ain't it great to be crazy!
Silly and foolish the whole day through,
Boom, boom, ain't it great to be crazy!

Way down south where bananas grow,
An ant stepped on an elephant's toe.
The elephant cried with tears in his
eyes,
"Why don't you pick on someone your
size?!" Refrain

A horse and a flea and three blind mice,
Sitting on a curbstone, shooting dice.
The horse, he slipped and fell on the
flea,
"Whoops!" said the flea, "There's a
horse on me!" Refrain

Way up north in the ice and snow,
There was a penguin, his name was Joe.
He got so sick of black and white,
He wore pink slacks to the dance
last night! Refrain

Why did the busy maggot fall asleep?

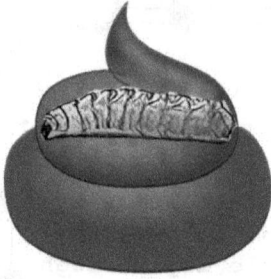

It was all pooped out.

**What did the
lawyer say when
a lady pushed
him down a manhole?**

Why did the gopher
play golf alone?

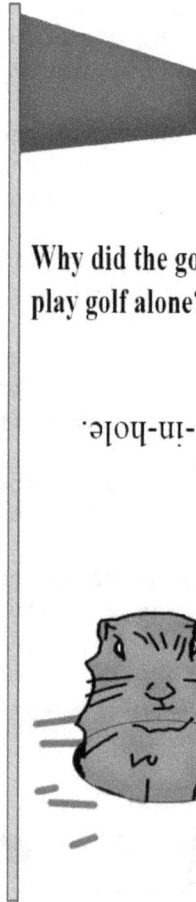

He wanted a
one-in-hole.

CITY SEWER

I'm going to sue her.

16

Latisha: Your name is mud.

Tom: No. My name is Tom.

Latisha: But, I'm going to drag your name through the mud.

Tom: That's impossible. You can't drag a word through mud.

Latisha: No, I'm a muck raker.

Tom: You mean a gardener?

Latisha: No, I'm going to sling mud at you.

Tom: I think I'd like to make a mud pie.

Latisha: It's not real mud.

Tom: Then how can you sling it? Or rake it? Or drag something through it?

Latisha: Stop muddying up the issue.

Tom: What's the issue?

Latisha: I'm going to make sure your name is mud.

Tom: Do you want to borrow my rake?

Latisha: Augh! I'm washing my hands of you.

Tom: You probably should since you like mud.

Where did the rat sleep on the ship?

On the poop deck.

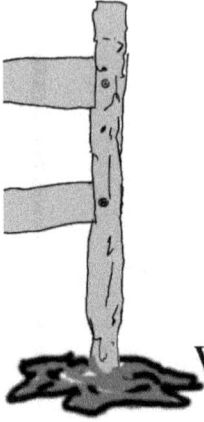

poop
deck

Why didn't the fence post like parties?

Because it was a old stick in the mud.

What kind of car do maggots like?

A Poop de Ville.

Dirty Jim

There was one little Jim,
'Tis reported of him,
And must be to his lasting disgrace,
That he was never seen
With hands at all clean
Nor yet ever clean was his face.

His friends were much hurt
To see so much dirt,
And often they made him quite clean;
But all was in vain,
He got dirty again,
And not at all fit to be seen.

It gave him no pain
To hear them complain,
Nor his own dirty clothes to survey;
His indolent mind
No pleasure could find
In tidy and wholesome array.

Mother Goose

Why did the audience boo the grubby magician?

They didn't
like his
dirty tricks.

What did the sink say to the broken toilet?

Urine it now.

A mud pile and a log pile had a race. Who won?

The mud pile
won by a
landslide.

Ten Little Angels
(Traditional)

Ten little angels
all dressed in white
tried to get to heaven
on the end of a kite.
The kite, it got broken.
Down they all fell.
Instead of going to
heaven
they all went to--

Nine little angels all dressed in white
tried to get to heaven on the end of a kite.
(Continue to one.)

One little angel all dressed in white
tried to get to heaven on the end of a kite.
The kite, it got broken. Down the angel fell.
Instead of going to heaven, she just went to
hello *(insert town or name here)*.

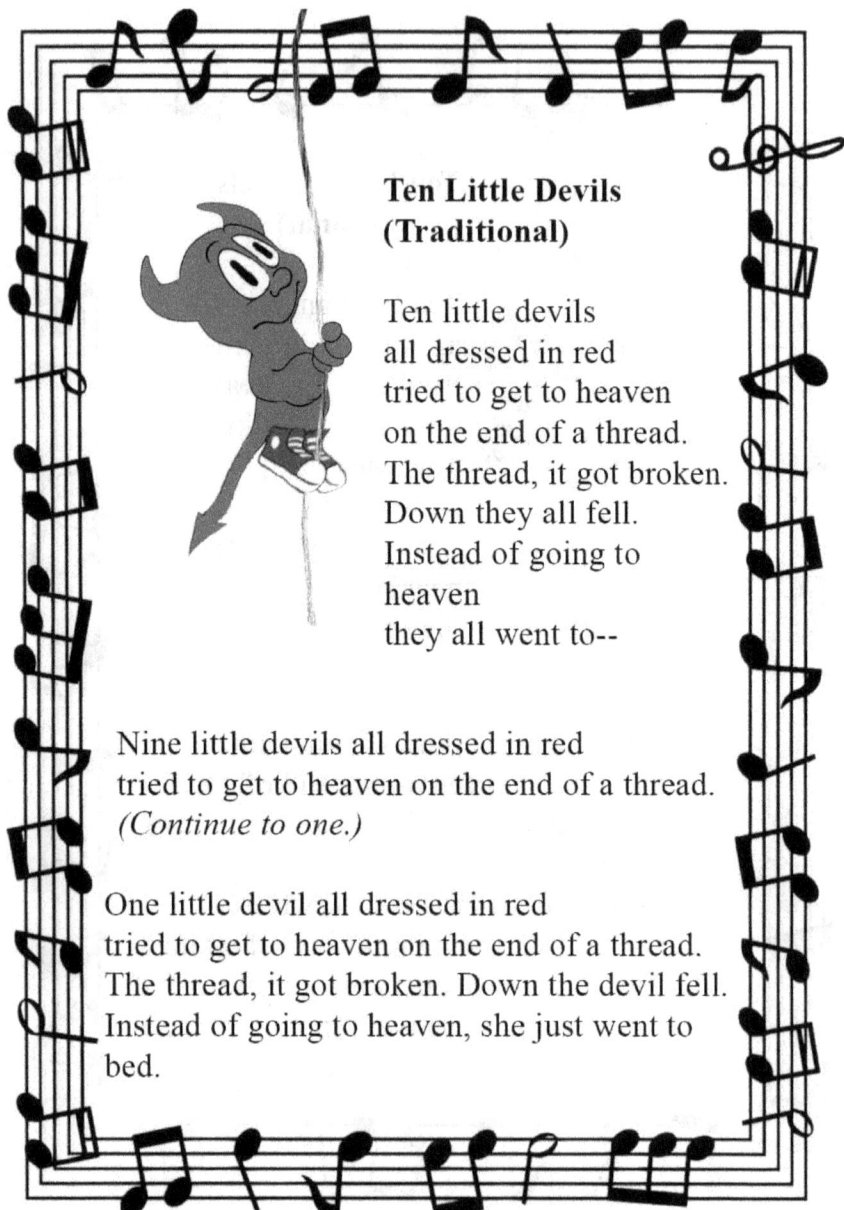

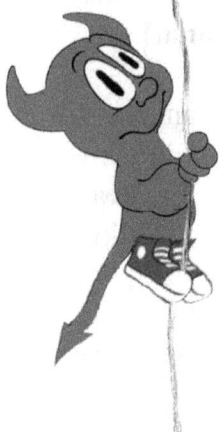

Ten Little Devils
(Traditional)

Ten little devils
all dressed in red
tried to get to heaven
on the end of a thread.
The thread, it got broken.
Down they all fell.
Instead of going to
heaven
they all went to--

Nine little devils all dressed in red
tried to get to heaven on the end of a thread.
(Continue to one.)

One little devil all dressed in red
tried to get to heaven on the end of a thread.
The thread, it got broken. Down the devil fell.
Instead of going to heaven, she just went to
bed.

NASTY FACT

Our guts are disgusting but what lives in them is really gross. There are millions of kinds of bacteria living in our gut along with fungi and viruses. Believe it or not, without some of them we couldn't be healthy.

(At least we can't see them.)

What dirty furry mammals live under your furniture?

Dust bunnies.

What's worse than eagles rising?

Seagulls dropping.

How did the cyclops face down the skunk?

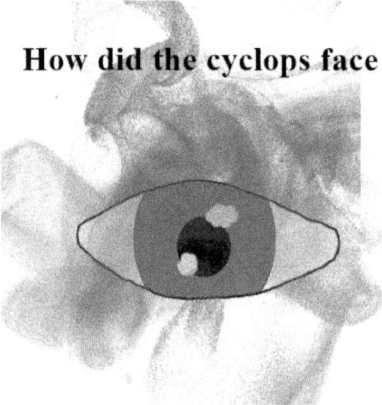

He gave him the stink eye.

What do you call a horse with diarrhea?

Whinny-the-poo.

Here I sit broken hearted.
Came to poop but only farted.

A toilet is the place where
some come to sit and think,
while others come to sit
and stink.

Why did mother wash her son's mouth out with soap after he denied playing in the mud?

SOAP

Because he was a dirty liar.

Why did the gassy child spin in circles?

She wanted to fart around.

Why did the frightened chicken stop in the middle of the road?

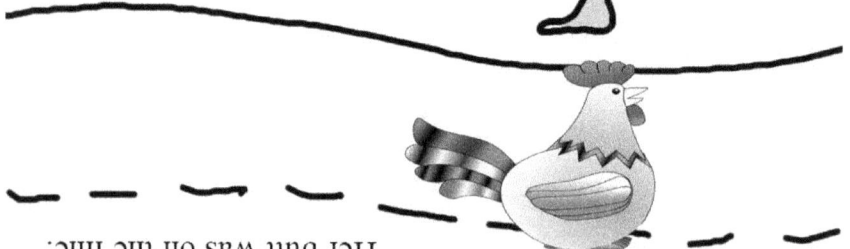

Her butt was on the line.

How do you stop a Jedi from stinking?

Give him dee-yoda-rant.

Why did the little league player wet the bed?

Because he was a pee wee.

How did the seasick sailor affect the captain?

He heaved too.

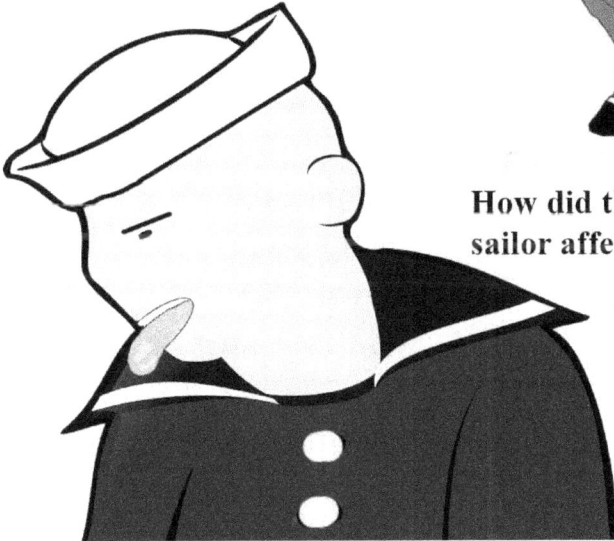

NASTY FACT

Dung beetles live on poop. They roll up balls of dung to store them for food and nesting. Some dung beetles can roll up a lot of balls the size of their bodies in just one night. Image rolling 250 balls. That's a lot of poop!

Dung beetles may be ugly and dirty, but they do us a favor. Imagine how much poop there would be if the dung beetles didn't process it down into usable nutrients. What would we do with it all?

Patience Is a Virtue

Patience is a virtue,

Virtue is a grace,

Grace is a little girl

Who wouldn't wash her face.

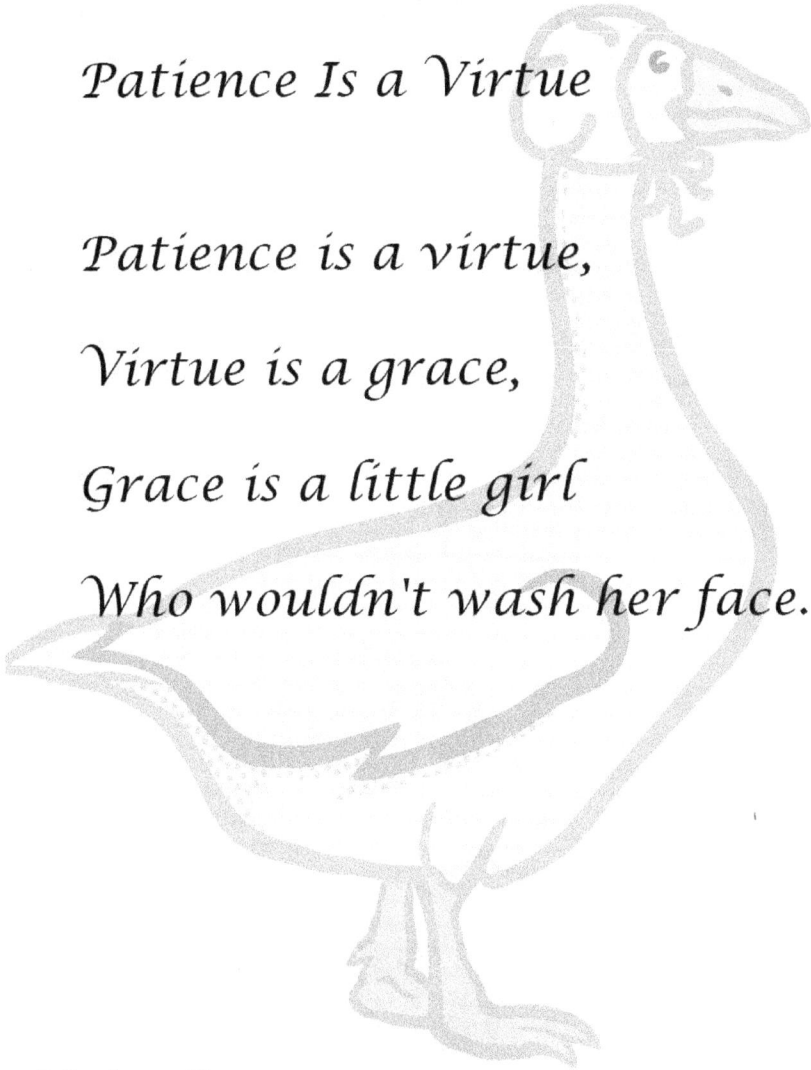

Mother Goose

Go Eat Worms (traditional)

Nobody likes me, everybody hates me.
Think I'll go eat worms.
Big fat juice ones. Long slimy skinny ones.
See how they wiggle and squirm.
First I bite the heads off.
Then I suck the guts out.
I throw the skins away.
Nobody knows how I survive
On worms three times a day.

Why do pigs gossip?

Because they love dirty secrets.

Why did the rabbit wear a hoodie?

He was having a bad hare day.

Why did the bloated man stop at the service station?

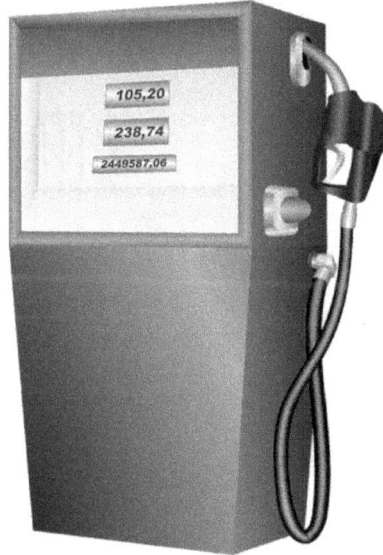

He didn't want to pass gas.

BIG BLACK BUGS BLEED
(TRADITIONAL TONGUE TWISTER)

BIG BLACK BUGS

BLEED BLACK BLOOD

BUT BABY BLACK BUGS

BLEED BLUE BLOOD

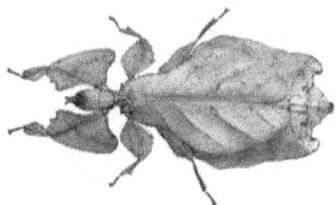

Why did the dummy take plastic dung into the bath?

Because it was sham-poo.

Why did no one want the dog?

Because he was a poo-dull.

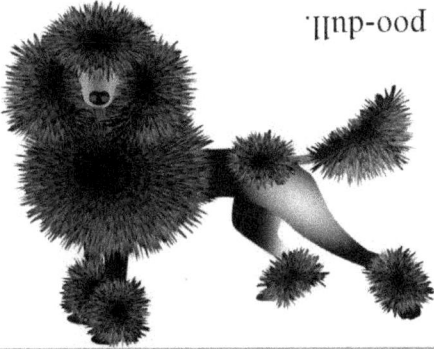

What did the race track say to the vacuum?

Eat my dust.

The KilKenny Cats

There were once two cats of KilKenny,
Each thought there was one cat too many;
So they fought and they fit,
And they scratched and they bit,
'Til, accepting their nails
And the tips of their tails,
Instead of two cats, there weren't any.

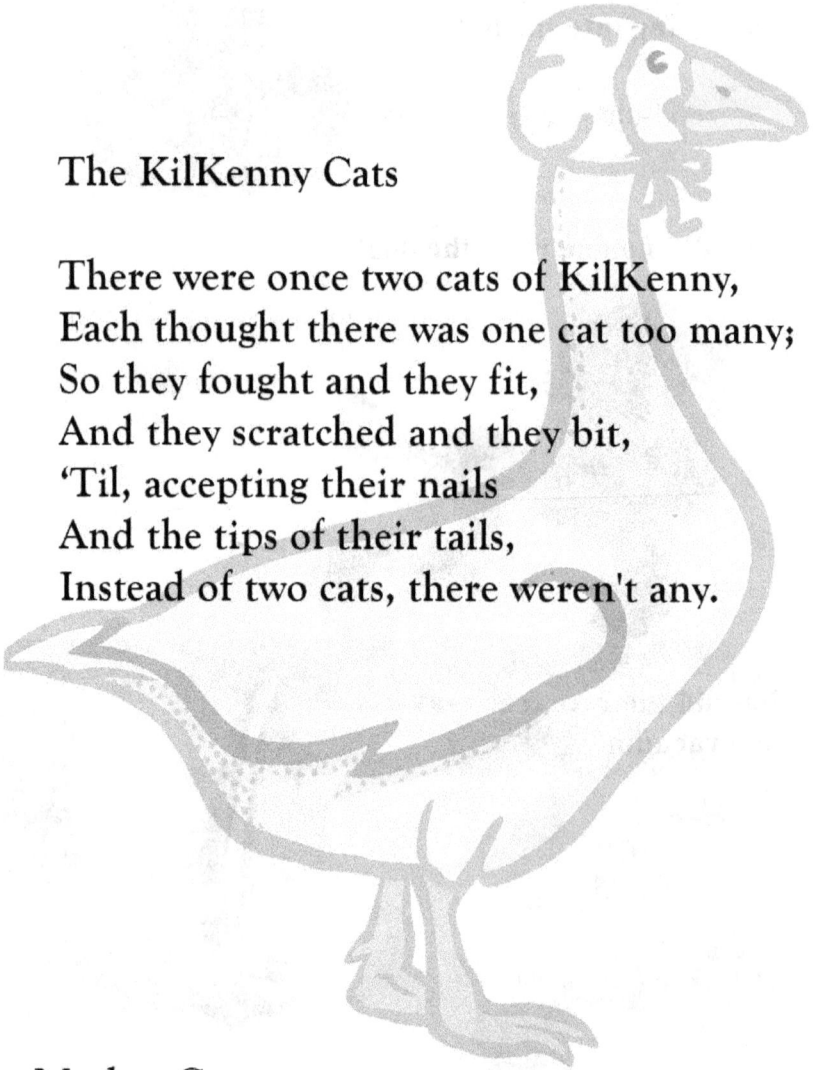

Mother Goose

NASTY FACTS

These are true ways people have used urine in history:

1. In Medieval times it was used to clean wounds.

2. One of the original ingredients in gunpowder was taken from urine.

3. In ancient times, urine was used to tan and lighten leather.

4. Urine has been used in fertilizer to help grow food.

5. Wool was soaked in urine in Scotland to make it ready for dying colors.

6. A few hundred years ago, urine was used for cleaning homes.

7. In ancient times, Romans used urine to clean their teeth!

(That new toothpaste flavor isn't so bad after all.)

Why did the nose go on strike?

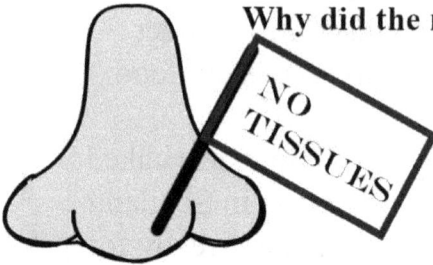

He liked to picket.

**What did Charlotte say to Templeton
when she was caught helping Wilbur?**

I smell a rat.

What do you call a baby straw with no diaper?

A pee shooter.

Three Jolly Fishermen (traditional)

There were three jolly fishermen, (2)
Fisher, fisher, men, men, men. (2)
There were three jolly fishermen.

The first one's name was Abraham (2)
Abra Abra ham ham ham (2)
The first one's name was Abraham

The second one's name was I-I-saac(2)
I-I I-I- saac saac saac (2)
The second one's name was I-I-saac

The third one's name was Ja-a-cob (2)
Ja-a Ja-a cob cob cob (2)
The third one's name was Ja-a-cob

They all went to Amster shhhhhh (2)
Amster Amster sh sh sh (2)
They all went to Amster sh

You mustn't say that naughty word (2)
We're going to say it anyway (2)
Amster Amster dam dam dam

**Why do angels farts
smell sweet?**

They can't stink
to high heaven.

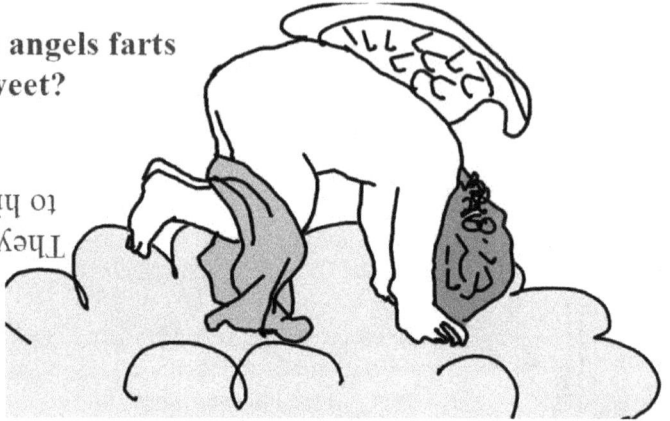

What kind of bath makes you dirty?

A mud bath.

My sister had
a mudpack facial.
She looked
great for three days.
Then the mud
fell off.

38

I'm Just a Little Puppy

I'm just a little puppy and as good as
can be,
And why they call me naughty I'm sure
I cannot see,
I've only carried off one shoe and torn
the baby's hat,
And chased the ducks and spilled the milk—
There's nothing bad in that!

Mother Goose

Why did everyone shop at the earthworm's store?

Because the prices were dirt cheap.

Why was the girl crying on the toilet?

Because she got dumped.

What was the soda pop's favorite exercise?

Burpees.

NASTY FACT

What furry pet leaves messages everywhere without writing a word?

Cats are the most frequent at spraying urine everywhere to say

"This couch is mine. Mine. Mine. Mine. Mine."

Why didn't the gargoyle spank his children?

Because he didn't want to hit rock bottoms.

Alex: Can I tell you something dirty?

Mimi: Okay.

Alex: A white horse fell in the mud.

Mimi: Can I tell you something dirtier?

Alex: Okay.

Mimi: He fell in the mud again.

Why was the frog a good baseball outfielder?

Because he loved catching flies.

Found a Peanut (traditional)

I found a peanut, found a peanut,
Found a peanut last night.
Last night I found a peanut,
Found a peanut last night.

I cracked it open, cracked it open ,
Cracked it open last night.
Last night I cracked it open,
Cracked it open last night.

It was rotten, it was rotten,
It was rotten last night.
Last night it was rotten,
It was rotten last night.

Ate it anyway, ate it anyway,
Ate it anyway last night.
Last night I ate it anyway,
Ate it anyway last night.

I got a fever, got a fever,
Got a fever last night.
Last night I got a fever,
Got a fever last night.

They didn't save me, didn't save me,
Didn't save me last night.
Last night they didn't save me,
Didn't save me last night.

I went up to heaven, went up to heaven,
Went up to heaven last night.
Last night I went up to heaven,
Went up to heaven last night.

The gates were locked tight,
The gates were locked tight,
The gates were locked tight last night.
Last night the gates were locked tight,
The gates were locked tight last night.

Went down to the other place last night.
Last night I went down to the other place.
Went down to the other place last night.

Was only dreaming, only dreaming,
Only dreaming last night.
Last night I was only dreaming.
Only dreaming last night.

I found a peanut, found a peanut,
Found a peanut last night.
Last night I found a peanut,
Found a peanut last night.

I cracked it open, cracked it open,
Cracked it open last night.
Last night I cracked it open,
Cracked it open last night.

It was rotten, it was rotten,
It was rotten last night.
Last night it was rotten,
It was rotten last night.

Ate it anyway!

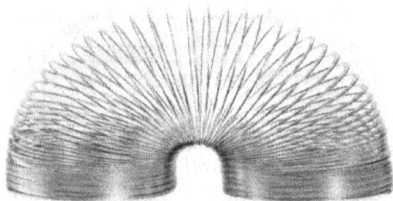

When should you wash a dirty slinky?

During spring cleaning.

What's the pig's favorite drinking toast?

Here's mud in your eye.

If dancing penguins have happy feet, what do dancing sewer rats have?

Stinky feet.

NASTY FACTS

How to Grow a Fart

Method One: Swallow a Lot of Air

Drink soda pop or other fizzy drinks.

Suck on a candy or an object.

Talk while you eat.

Method Two: Eat Fart Makers

Beans

Cabbage

Broccoli

Milk

Potatoes

Corn

Lentils

Wheat

There Was a Little Girl

There was a little girl, who had a little curl
Right in the middle of her forehead,
And when she was good, she was very,
very good.
But when she was bad, she was horrid.
She stood on her head, on her little
trundle bed,
With no one there to say, "no,"
She screamed and she squalled, she
yelled and she bawled,
And drummed her little heels against
the window.
Her mother heard the noise, and thought
it was the toys,
Falling in the dusty addict,
She rushed up the flight, and saw she
was alright,
And hugged her most emphatic.

Mother Goose

Where is my underwear?
I can't find any of mine.
Are they waiting in the dryer
Or waving on the line?
When will they be clean and dry?
When can they be worn?
Are they rotting in the washer
Forgotten and forlorn?

I ran out of paper towels
So I ripped them into shreds.
I used them to wax the car.
I scrubbed until the threads
Were worn thin and ragged
and frail as can be.
Now they're in the litter box
Soaking up the pee.

Great Green Globs of Gopher Guts (traditional)

Great green globs of greasy, grimy gopher guts,

Marinated monkey meat.

Dirty little birdie feet.

Great green globs of greasy, grimy gopher guts,

And me without my spoon.

Smell you later alligator

Pretty soon baboon

In a pig's eye dragonfly

Keep out of the mud rosebud

Don't cut the cheese busy bees

Stay out of the dump little chump

Avoid the trash succotash

Wipe your nose twinkle toes

Your turn

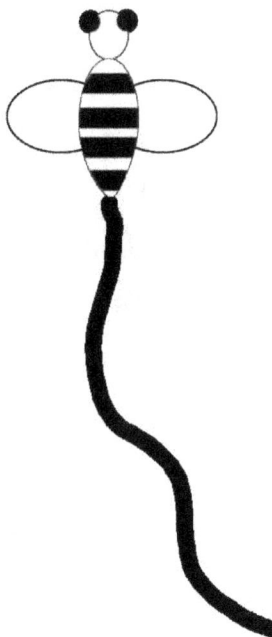

Goodbye (to the tune of Frère Jacques)

Now we're shared a silly song,
A grubby joke, and said so long.
Read them to your friend.
Don't let the laughter end.
You can't go wrong. You can't go wrong.